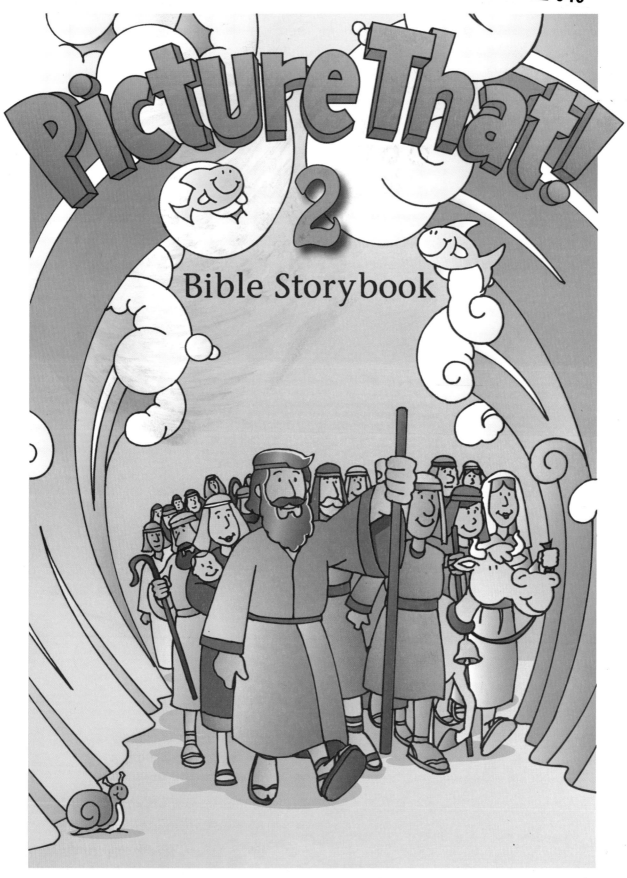

Picture That! 2

Bible Storybook

ZONDERkidz

 10 Commandments
 afraid
 angel
 animals
 ark
 ark

 Bible
 birds
 boat
 bread
 camels
 chariot

 cry
 desert
 Do not
 dog
 donkey
 down
 dream

 fish
 flies
 flowers
 food
 foot
 frog
 fruit

 heart
 heaven
 helmet
 horses
 house
 inn
 Israelites

 mad
 man
 money
 moon
 mountain
 nails
 net

 right
 river
 road
 rock
 roof
 sad
 salt

 stairs
 star
 statue
 stone
 stop
 storm
 strong

 treasure
 tree
 trumpet
 up
walk
wall

Woodson

 armor

 army

 axe

 baby

 baby Jesus

 basket

 children

 city

 cloud

 coat

 cow

cross

 drink

 ear

 eat

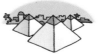 Egypt

 eyes

 feet

 fire

 garden

 giant

 girl

 go

 ground

 hair

 hand

 happy

 jail

 jar

 Jesus

 king

 light

 lion

 love

 night

 people

 Pharaoh

 pigs

 pray

 queen

 rain

 servant

 sheep

 shepherd

 sick

 sing

 snake

 staff

 sun

 sword

 table

 temple

 tent

 tomb

tower

 water

 wind

 window

 woman

 world

 worship

wrong

Dedication

To my —Amy, Lauren, and Ryan.

children

I you and I am 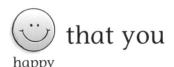 that you

love   happy   walk

in the .

light

ZONDERKIDZ

Picture That! 2 Bible Storybook
Previously published as *Amazing Stories of the Bible*
Copyright © 2002, 2011 by Tracy Harrast
Illustrations copyright © 2002, 2011 by Garry Colby

Requests for information should be addressed to:

Zondervan, *Grand Rapids, Michigan 49530*

Library of Congress Cataloging-in-Publication Data

Harrast, Tracy L.
    Picture That! 2, Bible storybook / by Tracy Harrast.
      p. cm.
    ISBN 978-0-310-72715-6 (softcover)
    1. Bible stories, English. I. Title.
  BS551.3.H356 2011
  220.9'505–dc22   2010052265

Editor: Gwen Ellis
Interior design: Jody DeNeef and Todd Sprague
Art direction: Michelle Lenger

Printed in China

11 12 13 14 15 /SCC/ 10 9 8 7 6 5 4 3 2 1

A Note to Moms & Dads

When I was five or six years old, I informed my mother: "I don't need to go to Sunday school anymore because I've already heard all of the Bible stories." I'm glad she kept taking me because, obviously, the Bible held much more to discover! This book tells many Bible stories that are amazing.

The little pictures within the text of this book not only add fun, they make reading easy for beginners. The first time my five-year-old son, Ryan, ever read a complete sentence was when he picked up from my desk the manuscript for my first storybook of this kind—*Picture That! Bible Storybook*. He beamed and said, "Hey, I can read this! I can read this!" I was thrilled to hear him sound out the simple words. Every time he came to a picture within the text, he smiled because he could guess the word it represented. The pictures in the sentences gave him the hints he needed for reading by himself.

I hope you'll feel the same joy as you hear your children read aloud these amazing stories simplified from God's Holy Word. It is my prayer that as you read together, you and your children will be awed by God's power and touched by his love.

Tracy L. Harrast

Old Testament

New Testament

Old Testament

Oh No! Sin Comes In

Genesis 1:1–3; Romans 5:1–21

God made the world and everything in it. The first

 people God made were Adam and Eve. God said

they could eat any fruit in the Garden of Eden

except **1**. Adam and Eve made the wrong choice. That

first sin changed the whole world ! Adam and Eve

had to leave the garden . After that, people would die

and have big problems. Many years later God would

send his Son Jesus to save people from sin and

death. When we believe  Jesus died on the cross to take the punishment for our sins, God will forgive us and will let us live forever in  heaven with him.

What Did You Learn?

Because Adam and Eve sinned, people die. Because Jesus gave his life, people can live forever.

The First Rainbow

Genesis 6:5–8:17

After a while, 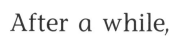 in the became so bad

people

world

that *every* thought they had was evil. God was very

. But there was **1** , Noah, who followed God.

sad

man

God told Noah to build a big . Then God sent

ark

at least **2** of every into the . After that,

animal

ark

it so much that covered the .

rained

water

earth

But God kept Noah, his family, and the safe

animals

in the . God promised that it would never

ark

4

 that much again. He put a rainbow in the

rain

sky as a reminder of his promise.

What Did You Learn?

Rainbows remind us that
God promised not to cover the
whole world with water again.

A Tower to Heaven

Genesis 11:1–9

When people first lived on the 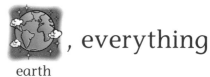, everything

earth

was new, all spoke the same language. When

people

they learned to make bricks, they became proud.

They tried to build a that would reach to

tower   up

. God did not want them to build the .

heaven   tower

To them, he changed their languages. They

stop

could not understand each other. So the building

came to a . When a babbles, no one

stop   baby

understands him. No one understood the people

when they talked, so they called the

 Babel.

city

What Did You Learn?

God wants us
to be humble.

Angels Come to Lunch

Genesis 18:1–15; 21:1–2

The Lord and **2** visited a named
angels   man

Abraham. Abraham told his wife, Sarah, "Quick!

Bake some !" He gave his a
bread   servant   cow

to fix for lunch. The ate the food. Then
angels

the told Abraham a secret. Sarah would
angels

have a within **1** year. Sarah laughed. She
baby

thought she was too old to have a . The Lord
baby

said, "Is anything too hard for God?" Sarah had the

 at the very time that the Lord had said.

baby

What Did You Learn?

Nothing is too hard for God.

A Woman Becomes Salt

Genesis 18:16–19:26

 in the of Sodom and the of Gomorrah did . God could not find **10** there who him enough to do what was .

 even tried to harm God sent there! came and led a named Lot and his family out of the . The warned, " look back and ." Then the cities caught on and burned to the ! Lot's wife did not obey. She looked back, and she became salt!

10

What Did You Learn?

When you are following God,
keep looking forward.

11

A Mean Wedding Trick

Genesis 29:1–30

Jacob fell in  **love** with a **woman** named Rachel who

took care of **sheep**. He worked **7** years for Rachel's

dad so he could marry Rachel. On their wedding

day, Jacob's bride wore a veil — a cloth that covered

her face. When the **sun** came **up** the next

morning, Jacob was surprised! His bride was not

Rachel! Her dad had tricked him! Jacob had

married the **wrong** **woman**, Rachel's sister, by mistake.

Jacob promised to work another **7** years so he

could marry Rachel.

What Did You Learn?

Be careful whom
you trust!

Joseph's Strange Dreams

Genesis 37:1–36;39:1–43:28

When Joseph was a boy, he had a **dream**. **11** **stars**,

the **sun**, and the **moon** all bowed **down** to him. God

told him the dream meant his whole family would

bow **down** to him someday. When Joseph told his

family about his dream, they were very angry! But

many years later when Joseph lived in Egypt, the  **Pharaoh**

had a **dream** of **7** skinny **cows** eating **7** fat  **cows**.

Joseph told **Pharaoh** that during **7** years when **food**

14

wouldn't grow, 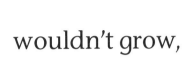 in 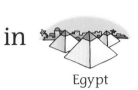 would  the

people Egypt   eat

 they had saved during **7** earlier years.

food   Pharaoh

then made Joseph a leader. And one day, Joseph's

family bowed to him, just like in his .

down   dream

What Did You Learn?

God knows what will happen
in the future.

God Splits the Water

Exodus 13:18–22;14

God led the (Israelites) through the  (desert). They

followed a (cloud) during the day and (fire) at (night).

 (Pharaoh) wanted the (Israelites) to come back to  (Egypt).

He and his (army) chased them! The (Israelites) could

not cross the Red Sea. So God made the (water) split!

The (Israelites) could  (walk) through on dry (ground).

They got away from (Pharaoh) and his (army)!

16

What Did You Learn?

God gets us through our troubles.

A Holdup Wins a Battle

Exodus 17:8–15

When an army attacked the  Israelites, Moses

stood on top of a hill with his staff in his  hands while

Joshua and some of the  Israelites fought the

 army. As long as Moses held  up his  hands, the

 Israelites won, but whenever he put down his hands,

they lost. When Moses' hands grew tired, he sat on

a stone. Aaron and Hur held his hands up **—1 on 1**

side, **1** on the other—till the sun went down. That is

how the  Israelites won the battle!

What Did You Learn?

We need to
help each other.

A House for God

Exodus 26–28; 1 Corinthians 6:19–20;
Hebrews 4:15–16; 6:19–20; 8:3–5, 9:11–14

God told the  to make a  called a

Israelites   tent

tabernacle where God would live. Later he had

Solomon build a to replace the tabernacle as

temple

God's home. The most holy room of the tabernacle

and held the that was like God's

temple   ark

throne in . Only the high priest could

heaven   go

into that room. was the last high priest. He

Jesus

made it so any **1** who believes in him can to
go

God's throne when we . In fact, God's Holy
pray

Spirit lives inside who believe in , so
people   Jesus

our bodies are now God's !
temple

What Did You Learn?

The tabernacle and temple were houses for God. Now our bodies are God's temple.

 A Talking Donkey

Numbers 22:21–33

1 morning a named Balaam got angry and hit

man

his for off the , for hurting

donkey   walking   road

Balaam's on a , and for lying . The

foot   wall   down

 talked! She said, "What have I done to make

donkey

you beat me?" The said, "You made a fool of

man

me!" He was angry that he couldn't make the

donkey

. Then the saw that an 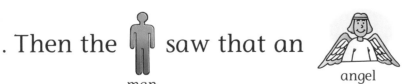 was in the

go   man   angel

with a drawn. The was the

road   sword   angel

reason the had to !

donkey   stop

What Did You Learn?

Sometimes angels are nearby
and we don't even know.

A Spy Mission

Numbers 13:1–27

God wanted to give some land to the .
Israelites

Moses sent as spies to look at the land. He
men   go

said, "See whether the who live there are
people

 or weak, few or many. Is their land good or
strong

bad? Do their have ? Will the
cities   walls

 grow plants? Are there ? Do
ground   trees

your best to bring back some of the land."
fruit

They looked at the land for **40** days. **2** of the

came back carrying a huge bunch of

grapes on a pole between them. They told Moses

and the , "The land does flow with milk

and honey! Here is its ."

fruit

What Did You Learn?

God gives good gifts
to his children.

25

You Want to Go Where?

Numbers 13:28–14:34

God wanted the  Israelites to move into the good

land that the spies had seen. Caleb said, "We should

 go take the land!" The other spies said, "We can't.

We're not as strong as the giants there." That night

the Israelites complained, "We should go back to

 Egypt ." Joshua said, " Do not rebel against God."

The people wanted to throw stones at Joshua

Moses, and Aaron! Then Moses saw a light , and

God said, "How long will they treat me like they

hate me? Why won't they believe in me?" Because

of his  love , God forgave the Israelites , but because

they complained so much, they would have to

walk around lost in the desert for **40** years.

What Did You Learn?

Don't complain about God's plans.

 Just Look and Live

Numbers 21:6–10, John 3:14–16

While the  Israelites were in the  desert,

 snakes bit them and many died. The Israelites

asked Moses to pray. God told Moses to make a

bronze snake and put it on a pole. When any **1**

who had been bitten by a snake looked at the

bronze snake, he lived. All the others died. The

 Bible says to lift up Jesus like Moses lifted

28

the bronze  so that any **1** who believes in

snake

 will live forever. God loved the so

Jesus   world

much that he gave his **1** and only Son that whoever

believes in will not die but will live forever.

Jesus

What Did You Learn?

If we show Jesus to people,
they can look to him and live.

Aaron's Staff Blooms

Numbers 1:50; 17:1—11

Some  (Israelites) didn't believe God put the Levites in

charge of the tabernacle. They were angry with

Moses and his brother Aaron. God told Moses, "Get **1**

🦯(staff) from the leader of each of the **12** tribes and write

each man's name on his 🦯(staff)." Aaron was from Levi's

tribe, so his name was on the Levite 🦯(staff). Moses said that

the staff belonging to the 👤(man) God chose would sprout.

The very next day, Aaron's 🦯(staff) not only sprouted, but

it budded, blossomed, and grew almond nuts!

30

What Did You Learn?

God cared about who was in charge of his tabernacle.

An Ark That Wasn't a Boat

Exodus 25:1–22 ; Deuteronomy 10:55; Psalm 99:1; 1 Chronicles 13:9–10;
Joshua 3:15–17; 1 Samuel 5:9–10; Hebrews 4:14–16; 9:4

Unlike Noah's  , the in the was a

ark   ark   temple

wooden box covered with gold. Its lid was called

"the mercy seat." It was like God's throne. Carved

 on the lid looked like those who worship

angels

God in . The  held the , some

heaven   ark   10 Commandments

manna, and Aaron's that bloomed. As

staff   Israelites

carried the into the Jordan , the

ark   River   water

32

split so they could through on dry . Once

go · ground

when a man touched the , he died instantly.

ark

Another time, an  stole the and got

army · ark

lumps under their skin. They quickly gave the ark

back to the . Solomon put the in the

Israelites · ark

holiest room of the .

temple

What Did You Learn?

The ark reminded the Israelites that God was with them.

Joshua's Amazing Battles

Joshua 1:1–24:24

God made the   so Joshua could lead the

river   stop

 across on dry into Canaan. God

Israelites   ground

promised, "I will give you every place where you set

your ." Remember how God made a

foot   wall

fall and how he made the   so

down   sun   stop

Joshua's

army

could win battles

for the Promised

Land? When a

bad tried to run away from Joshua, God

sent big hailstones from the ! The

hailstones killed more of the bad than the

 of the  did! Joshua reminded his

, "It was God who fought for you." He got

them to promise that they would serve and obey

God. He gave each family part of the

Promised Land.

What Did You Learn?

God gives what he promises.

The Moldy Bread Trick

Joshua 9

To get the  Israelites to promise not to fight them,

the Gibeonites pretended to live farther away than

they really did. They loaded  donkeys with

worn-out sacks, put patched sandals on their

 feet , wore old clothes, and brought bread that

was dry and green with mold to Joshua. They lied

and said these had all been new when they began

their trip. The  Israelites did not pray about what to

do. They wrote down a promise that they would not

fight the Gibeonites. When they learned about the

trick, they didn't fight. Instead, they used the

Gibeonites for  .

servants

What Did You Learn?

We need to pray
before we make
decisions.

Amazing Deborah Wins a War

Judges 4

A woman named Deborah was an  Israelite leader.

She decided who was right and who was wrong. **1**

day she told Barak, "God says to take an  army

to a mountain where God will put the other army's

leader into your hands." Barak would not go

without Deborah. She said, "I will go with you,

but if you ⊘ do not do this the way God said, the honor

will not be yours. God will hand that leader to a

woman

." Deborah and Barak's  won, but a
army

woman

named Jael, instead of Barak, was the **1** who

killed the other army's leader.

What Did You Learn?

It would be a shame if we didn't obey God
and he had to use someone else.

Surprising Signs for Gideon

Judges 6

An  angel told Gideon to lead the  Israelites in a

battle. Gideon wanted to be sure this was what God

wanted and that God would help him. Gideon said to

God, "I will place a fleece outside. If there is dew only

on the fleece and all the ground is dry, I will know

that you will save the  Israelites." The next morning

the fleece was wet and the ground was dry! Gideon

prayed , "Let me ask for **1** more test. This time make

the fleece dry and the covered with dew."

ground

The next morning the fleece was dry and the

 was wet!

ground

What Did You Learn?

It is important that we try to find
God's will for our lives.

The Incredible Shrinking Army

Judges 7:1–22

God wanted the army men to know that when

they won a battle it was through his help, not just

because they had many strong men. God told

Gideon to send home any **1** in the army who was

 afraid to fight. Then he told Gideon to take the men

who were left to get a drink at the river. God told

Gideon to send home the men who got down on

their knees to drink water. Gideon only kept **300**

who lapped with their to their mouths.

men

hands

Then God told Gideon's small  how to win.

army

They blew trumpets, broke , held torches,

jars

and shouted. The other fought themselves

army

by mistake, , and ran away!

cried

What Did You Learn?

God is our strength.

Samuel Picks the Little Guy

1 Samuel 16:1–13

Samuel had to find out which of Jesse's sons God

wanted to be 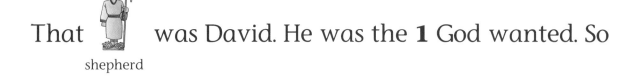 king . God said, " Ø Do not think about how

he looks or how tall he is. Man looks at the outside, but

God looks at the heart ." Samuel met **7** of Jesse's sons

and knew God had not chosen any of them. Then

Jesse said his youngest son was taking care of sheep .

That shepherd was David. He was the **1** God wanted. So

Samuel put drops of oil on David to show that he

44

would be  . Later, David fought a and won.

Then after many years, he became .

What Did You Learn?

God looks at the heart.

Saul's Close Calls

1 Samuel 24; 26:5–25; 1 Chronicles 10:4–14

1 day while David was playing the harp for King

Saul, Saul threw a spear at David! David ran away.

For a long time, King Saul and his  army chased

David and planned to kill him. **1** time Saul came

into a cave and didn't see David in the dark.

David cut off a corner of Saul's coat to prove to

Saul that he had passed up a chance to kill him.

Later David found Saul asleep with his spear stuck in

the ground near his head. He took the spear to prove

46

he had shown mercy to Saul again. Later  Saul

died, and David became the .

What Did You Learn?

God doesn't want us to take revenge.

David Helps a Lame Guy

2 Samuel 9

 Saul's son, Jonathan, was David's very close

friend. After Saul and Jonathan died, David

became . He asked, "Is any **1** left in Saul's

family to whom I can show kindness for Jonathan's

sake?" A said, "Jonathan's son is alive. He is

crippled in both 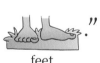." David gave the lame

son land and after that always let him at

his like **1** of his sons. The lame asked,

48

"Why should you notice a dead  like me?"

David showed kindness like God does. We're like the

 who felt as worthless as a dead . God wants

us at his in as his !

What Did You Learn?

Show kindness like God does.

49

Who's the Real Mom?

1 Kings 3:16–28

 Solomon asked God for wisdom, and God gave

it. **1** day **2** came to see Solomon. They

both said they were **1** baby's mother. The

pretended he thought the should be cut in **2**

pieces so half of the could go to each . The

real mom her . She said, "Give the

to her! Don't kill him!" Then the knew who

the real mom was. He let the live, and gave

him to the who wanted him to be safe. The

woman

 saw that the had wisdom from God

Israelites   king

to do what was and fair.

right

What Did You Learn?

Wisdom comes from God.

The Incredible Expanding Food

1 Kings 17:1–16

During a time when no fell for years, there

rain

was not much or . God sent **black**

food water

 to bring and meat to Elijah **2**

birds bread

times each day. Then God told a to share with

woman

him. When Elijah asked her for a of

drink water

and a piece of , she told him, "I only have

bread

a little flour and oil." She thought the flour and oil

would make her last meal for her son and herself

before they starved. The shared with Elijah

woman

anyway, and the flour and oil did not run out until

God sent .

rain

What Did You Learn?

God blesses us when we do what he asks.

Woodson

1 Kings 18:16–40

Elijah said to who  a 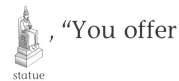 , "You offer

people · worshiped · statue

meat to your god. I'll offer meat to my God. The god

who catches the meat on is real." The

fire · people

 to the , but no **1** answered. Elijah teased,

prayed · statue

"Maybe he is asleep." Then Elijah to the real

prayed

God, "I did what you said. Answer me so these

people

will know you're God and you're turning their

hearts

back again." Then came and burned the

fire · down · up

meat, the wood, and even around it! The

water · people

fell and , "The Lord is God!"

down · cried

54

What Did You Learn?

God wants people
to know he is real.

Three Thirsty Kings

2 Kings 3

After **3**  kings marched for **7** days with their army, they had no more water for themselves or their animals. **1** king asked

Elisha for help. Elisha told him, "God says to make

this valley full of ditches. You will see neither

 nor , yet this valley will be filled

wind   rain

with . You, your , and your other

water   cows

 will . This is easy in the of the

animals   drink   eyes

Lord. You will win your battle too." The next

morning, flowing filled the valley. Then the

water

3 won the battle just as God said they would.

kings

What Did You Learn?

Amazing miracles are easy for the Lord.

The Miraculous Oil Jar

2 Kings 4:1–7

A could not repay she owed to some

woman   money

. They wanted to take her sons and make

people

them work as . She turned to Elisha for help.

servants

He asked, "What do you have in your ?" She

house

said, "Just a little oil." Elisha said, " ask neighbors

Go

for empty . Ask for many. Then inside,

jars   go

shut the , and pour oil into all the ."

door   jars

The of oil kept pouring until there were no

jar

left to fill. Then the oil stopped flowing.

jars

Elisha said, " , sell the oil, and pay the  you

Go

money

owe. You and your sons can live on the  that

money

is left."

What Did You Learn?

We can trust God to take care of us.

An Axe Head Floats

2 Kings 6:1–7

A **man** named Elisha listened to God. He and his

friends wanted to build a meeting place near the

Jordan **River** , so they got to work. They chopped

down **trees** with an **axe** . As **1** **man** was cutting

down a **tree** , the metal part of the **axe** fell into the

water and sank. "Oh no!" he **cried** out, "I had

borrowed that **axe** !" Elisha cut a stick and threw

it where the **axe** head had fallen. That made the

heavy metal part of the float! "Lift it out,"

axe

Elisha said. Then the reached out his and

man   hand

took it.

What Did You Learn?

God even cares about our little problems.

Chariots of Fire to the Rescue

2 Kings 6:8–23

When Elisha's servant got up **1** morning, he saw an evil king's

 army , horses , and  chariots around the city . The

 servant was afraid . Elisha prayed, "O Lord, open his eyes so he

may see." Then the servant saw the hills full of horses and

 chariots made of fire all around! As the bad army

came toward him, Elisha prayed , "Strike them blind." The

 army could not see! Elisha led them to another city .

Then when he asked God to open their eyes , they could see

again. Elisha let the army go back to their king .

What Did You Learn?

Sometimes we can't see
all of the help God has sent.

An Eight-Year-Old King

2 Kings 22:1–23:30

Josiah was **8** years old when he became . He

king

did what was . He had workers fix the .

right   temple

They found part of the that no **1** had read

Bible

for a long time. Josiah felt that his

King   sad   people

had not obeyed what the said. Josiah

Bible   King

told God he was sorry, and he . Because the

cried

 , God put a to his plans to destroy

king prayed   stop

their land.  Josiah read the aloud to his

King   Bible

people

. They promised to follow God and keep his

commands with all of their and soul.
heart

What Did You Learn?

A leader who loves
God can turn his
people away
from evil.

A Shadow Creeps Backward

2 Kings 20:1–11, 20

A 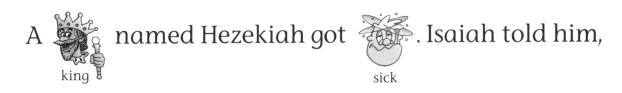 named Hezekiah got ⬦. Isaiah told him,

king **sick**

"The Lord says to get ready because you will die."

Hezekiah ⬦ and ⬦. After Isaiah left the palace,

prayed **cried**

God sent him back to tell the  that God said, "I

king

heard you ⬦ and saw you ⬦. I will heal you. I

pray **cry**

will add **15** years to your life. And I will not let the

 of Assyria rule over you." Hezekiah asked how

king

he could be sure. Isaiah 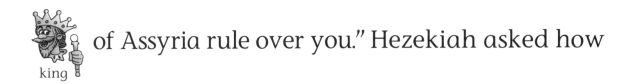 for the shadow on the

prayed

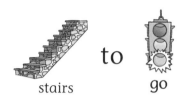
stairs

to  backwards up the **10**  it

go

stairs

had already gone ⬇, and that's what happened!

down

What Did You Learn?

God is in charge of how long we live.

A Praying Queen Foils a Plot

Esther 1–10

A bad man named Haman got a king to say that all

the Jews would be killed. The king did not know

that his wife, a queen named Esther, was Jewish.

 Queen Esther wanted to stop Haman's evil plan, but a

 queen could be killed if she went to see the king when

he had not called for her. Her uncle said to her, "Who

knows, but maybe you have become the queen for

such a time as this?" Queen Esther asked the Jews to

68

fast—not or —for **3** days. After **3** days,

 Esther went to see the . He was glad to see

her! The let the Jews live. He had bad Haman

killed instead.

What Did You Learn?

It is good to pray and
fast with friends about
big problems.

It Couldn't Get Much Worse

Job 1–42

A (man) named Job (prayed) often and did (right). God let

Satan tempt Job. (Fire) killed his (sheep) and (servants).

His (camels) were stolen. (Wind) blew (down) a (house),

killing his (children). Job bowed to the (ground) in

(worship). He said, "The Lord gave and the Lord has

taken away." Then sores covered Job, but Job didn't

sin. He said, "Should we take good from God and not

trouble?" Friends said he must have sinned to

deserve all this. God said Job's friends were .

wrong

He gave Job twice what he had before.

What Did You Learn?

Trust God even in hard times,
and don't blame people
when bad things happen to them.

New Testament

 Christmas Angels

Luke 1:26–39; Matthew 1:18–21

1 day an angel surprised a young woman named

Mary. He said, "You will have a baby . Name him

 Jesus ." The angel explained, "He will be the Son

of God. Nothing is impossible with God." An angel

came to Joseph, the man who was engaged to Mary.

The angel said in a dream , " Do not be afraid to take

Mary as your wife. Name the baby Jesus because he

will save people from their sins." When baby Jesus was

74

born, an said to some , "A Savior has

angel

shepherds

been born to you! He is Christ the Lord. Suddenly

a large group of  from  also

angels

heaven

appeared and praised God!

What Did You Learn?

Jesus is the Son of God,
and he saves us
from our sins.

God Speaks Up for His Son

Matthew 17:1–8; 3:16–17; John 12:20–28

God spoke from  the day Jesus was

heaven

baptized and said, "This is my Son, whom I ;

love

I am well pleased with him." God said the same

thing from a  while and **3** friends

cloud   Jesus

were on a . That day God added, "Listen to

mountain

him!" Jesus' friends were so , they fell on

afraid   down

the . On another day, told friends he

ground   Jesus

would die on the soon and receive glory. He

cross

76

said, "Father, glorify your name!" A voice from

heaven

said, "I have glorified it, and will glorify it

again."

What Did You Learn?

God loves his Son Jesus and is pleased
with him. He wants us to listen to him.

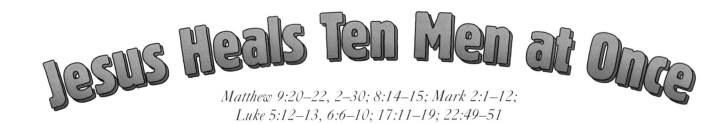

Jesus Heals Ten Men at Once

Matthew 9:20–22, 2–30; 8:14–15; Mark 2:1–12;
Luke 5:12–13, 6:6–10; 17:11–19; 22:49–51

One day **10** men with a skin disease called loudly,

" Jesus , Master, have pity on us!" Jesus said, " Go show

yourself to the religious leaders." And as they went,

Jesus made their skin disease disappear! One man

came back praising God loudly. He threw himself at

the feet of Jesus and thanked him. Jesus asked,

"Weren't all **10** cleansed? Where are the other **9**?"

Then he said to the man , "Get up and go ; your faith

has made you well." Jesus healed the eyes of blind

men. He helped lame men to  walk.  Jesus touched

the hand of a woman with a fever and the fever left.

 Jesus said to a man whose hand was shriveled, "Stretch

out your hand." He did and his hand was normal!

What Did You Learn?

Jesus cares when we're sick, and he wants us to thank him when he heals us.

Back to Life

Luke 7:11–17; 8:49–9:1, John 11:1–46

Jesus

brought some people back to life after they

died. When he saw a dead man carried out of the

 city , Jesus felt sad for the man's mom and said

to her, "Don't cry ." Jesus told the dead man to get up .

The man sat up and began talking! After a 12-year-

old girl died, Jesus took her hand and said, "My child,

get  up !" She did! After Lazarus had been in a

 tomb for **4** days, Jesus said to the man's sister,

"I am the resurrection and the life. Whoever believes

in me will live, even though he dies." After the stone

was moved from the doorway of the  tomb , Jesus

called to the dead man , "Lazarus, come out!" Every

1 was amazed when Lazarus  walked out of

the  tomb .

What Did You Learn?

Jesus has power over
life and death.

Jesus—A Good Friend to Bad People

Matthew 9:9–13; Mark 2:13–17;
Luke 5:27–32; John 8:1–11; Luke 7:36–50

1 time, caught a doing . They brought her to
people   woman   wrong

 and wanted to throw at her. said, "If
Jesus   stones   Jesus

any of you is without sin, let him be the first to throw a ."
stone

Every **1** left except the and . He told her, "I
woman   Jesus   do not

want you to be punished. and leave your life of sin."
Go

Another day, a who had been sinful came to . She
woman   Jesus

 on his and wiped them with her . Jesus said,
cried   feet   hair

"Her many sins have been forgiven because she much.
loved

But he who has been forgiven little little."
loves

82

What Did You Learn?

Jesus loves us
even when we
have done wrong.

Love Your Enemies

Matthew 5:44–48; 22:37–40; John 13:34, 35

Jesus
said loving God and other

people
are the

greatest commands. Every command in the

Bible
is about showing

love
.

Jesus
said to

even

love
your enemies and

pray
for those who

are mean to you. After all, God makes his

sun
rise

on both the evil and the good,

and he sends

rain
on both

those who do

right
and those

who do . We are not just supposed to

wrong

love

those who us or only say hello to friends and

love

family. Even without God do that.

people

Jesus

said, "As I have loved you, so you must

love

1 another. This is how all men will know that you

learn from me, if you **1** another."

love

What Did You Learn?

God wants us to love everyone
like he does.

What Is Most Valuable

Matthew 19:16–26; 13:45–46

 said, "The kingdom of  is like a

Jesus   heaven

salesman who looked for fine pearls. When he found

1 of great value, he sold everything he had and

bought the pearl." The kingdom of God was worth

more than what the man gave  for it.

up   Jesus

asked a young ruler who had a lot of to sell all

money

he had and give to the poor so he would have

treasure

in . Instead, the went away . He

heaven   man   sad

made the  choice. Disciples of  made the

right  choice. They even away

walked

from their jobs to follow .

Jesus

What Did You Learn?
Following Jesus as King is worth more than anything.

How Many Hairs Do You Have?

Matthew 6:25–30; 10:28–3; Luke 15:3–24; James 4:8

You matter very much to God. said that if **1**

 falls to the , God knows about it.

bird · ground

And you are worth more than the  . He

birds

said even the hairs of your head are counted! God

feeds the and clothes the , so you

birds · flowers

can trust him to feed and clothe you. If you ever

wandered away from God, he would look for

you like a looks for his lost . told

shepherd · sheep · Jesus

about a runaway son who did  things. The
wrong

son wanted to come home, but he was his dad
afraid

would be very . Instead, the dad ran out to hug
mad

him! God feels that

way about you!

What Did You Learn?

We matter very much to God!

Peter Starts to Walk by Faith

Matthew 8:23–27; 14:22–33; 15:32–38; Luke 5:1–11; John 21:1–14

 Jesus did many miracles. He fed thousands of people with only

1 boy's lunch. He filled nets with fish . He even calmed a

 storm instantly! On another night , Jesus walked on water

across the sea to friends who were on a boat . Peter wanted to

 walk on the sea too. When Jesus said to him, "Come," Peter

did. But as soon as Peter saw the wind , he became afraid and

began to sink. Peter cried , "Lord, save me!" Jesus caught him by

the hand and said, "You of little faith, why did you doubt?" When

they climbed into the boat , the people in the boat

worshiped Jesus saying, "Truly you are the Son of God."

90

What Did You Learn?

Jesus can do what
seems impossible, so
walk by faith and
don't let doubts pull
you down.

Runaway Pigs

Mark 5:1–20

A 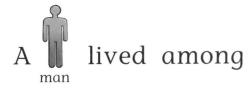 lived among  tombs. No **1** was strong

enough to control him. He broke chains, cried out,

and cut himself with stones. When he saw Jesus,

he fell on his knees and shouted, "What do you

want with me, Jesus, Son of God?" Jesus said,

"Come out of him, you evil spirit!" The many evil

spirits that were in the man went out of him and

into a herd of about **2,000** pigs. The pigs

92

rushed  the hill into the lake and drowned.

down

Now the 🧍 was fine. Jesus said, "🚦 tell your

man

Go

family how much the Lord has done for you."

What Did You Learn?

Jesus is stronger than evil.

A Fish Delivers a Coin

Matthew 17:24–27

Where Jesus lived, people paid money called taxes

to take care of the temple and its workers. Someone

asked Peter, "Doesn't Jesus pay the temple tax?"

Peter said, "Yes, he does." When Peter came into the

 house , Jesus was the first to speak. He asked, "Do

kings of the world collect

taxes from their

own sons or

94

others?" Peter said, "From others." "Then the sons

do not
have to pay,"  said. "But so that we
Jesus

may not upset them, to the lake and throw your
go

line into the water . Take the first fish you catch;

open its mouth and you will find a coin. Give it to

them for our tax."

What Did You Learn?

God can give us what we need ...
even in unusual ways.

Jesus Puts Back an Ear

Luke 22:39–54

Jesus went to a to . He wanted to be
mountain   pray

ready for the time when he would die on a .
cross

After  , a mob showed up who wanted to
Jesus prayed

take him away. Jesus' friend Peter wanted to
stop

them. He lifted a and cut off the right of a
sword   ear

 named Malchus. Jesus said, "No more of this!"
servant

He touched the man's and healed him.
ear

What Did You Learn?

Jesus even helped people
who wanted to harm him.

The Day Jesus Died

Matthew 27:50–61; Mark 15:37–16:1;
Luke 23:44–56; John 19:38–42

When died on the , many amazing

Jesus — cross

events happened. The stopped shining. The

sun

 curtain, which had separated from

temple — people

God, tore apart. The shook,  split,

ground — rocks

and broke open. After Jesus rose, bodies

tombs

of holy who had died came to life and went

people

into the ! When the guards saw the

city

earthquake and all that happened, they were

afraid

and said, "Surely was the Son of God!" Joseph

Jesus

of Arimathea took the body of   from

Jesus   down

the . With the help of a named Nicodemus,

cross   man

Joseph put the body of  in a that

Jesus   tomb

had never been used.

What Did You Learn?

Surely Jesus is
the Son of God.

99

Jesus Appears

Luke 24:13–53

While **2** men were on the road to Emmaus,

 Jesus began to walk with them. They didn't

recognize him. They told him, "Our rulers put

 Jesus on a cross **3** days ago. Women went to the

 tomb but didn't find his body. They told us

 angels said he was alive. Our friends went to the

 tomb ,but they did not see Jesus ."  Jesus said,

"You are slow to believe all the  says! Christ

Bible

had to suffer these things." Then the invited

men

Jesus into their . He sat at their , ,

house   table   prayed

and handed them some . That's when they

bread

saw that he was , and then he disappeared!

Jesus

Many others saw alive too.

Jesus

What Did You Learn?

Jesus is alive! He did what the Bible said
he would do.

The Sewing Lady Comes Back

Acts 9:36–41

A named Tabitha sewed clothes for a living.
woman

She did good and helped who didn't have
people

enough . **1** day Tabitha became and died.
money   sick

Some who followed said to Peter,
people   Jesus

"Please come at once!" When Peter went into the

room where Tabitha's body was, he saw .
women crying

They showed him the clothes Tabitha had made

while she was still alive. Peter sent them out. Then he

got  on his knees to . He turned toward the

dead and said, "Tabitha, get ." She opened

her and sat ! Peter took her and

helped her to her . Many  in the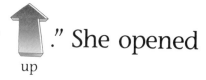

heard about this and believed in .

What Did You Learn?

When people hear about the
great things God has done,
many believe in him.

Two Liars Drop Dead

Acts 4:32–5:12

After Jesus went to heaven, his followers shared

all they had. No **1** was needy, because from time to

time, people who sold their land or houses brought

the money to the apostles. Then those leaders gave

the money to whoever had a need. Ananias and his

wife, Sapphira, sold some land, but kept part of the

 money. Then they brought the rest to the leaders as if

it was all of the money. Peter said, "You have not lied

to men but to God." Ananias fell dead.

down   Men

carried him out and buried him. His wife came in

later and lied too. Peter said, "The of the

feet

 who buried your husband are at the . They

men   door

will carry you out also." Then she fell at his

down

 dead. buried her beside her husband.

feet   Men

What Did You Learn?

God knows the truth.

Angel Power Opens a Gate

Acts 12:1–17

 Herod put Peter in for telling about .

King · jail · people · Jesus

The of the church began to for Peter. While Peter

people · pray

was asleep and chained between **2** soldiers, an came.

angel

The woke him. "Quick, get !" he said. The chains fell

angel · up

off Peter's wrists. Then the told him to put on clothes

angel

and follow him. Peter followed the out of . The

angel · jail

gate leading to the opened by itself. Then the

city · angel

left. Peter went to a where many were . He

house · people · praying

told them how God had brought him out of .

jail

What Did You Learn?

God can lead us out of our problems.

Philip Disappears!

Acts 8:26–9:1–40

An  (angel) told Philip to (walk) (down) a (road)

through the (desert). There he saw an African  (man)

riding a (chariot). The spirit told Philip, " (Go) to

that (chariot)." Philip ran to it and heard the (man)

reading the (Bible). "Do you understand it?"

Philip asked. The (man) said, "I need someone to

explain it." He asked Philip to sit with him. Philip

said the verse was about (Jesus). When they came

to some 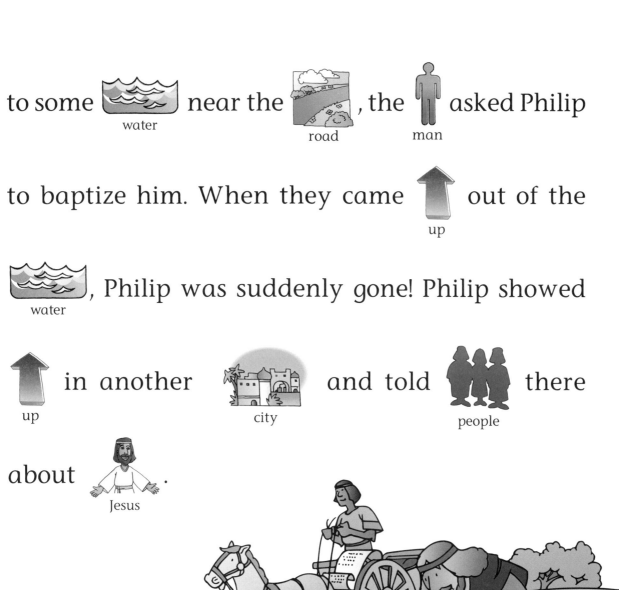 water near the road, the man asked Philip

to baptize him. When they came up out of the

water, Philip was suddenly gone! Philip showed

up in another city and told people there

about Jesus.

What Did You Learn?

God can put us in the right place
at the right time to tell about Jesus.

Stephen Sees Right into Heaven

Acts 6:1–8:3

Stephen helped the church give to widows.

Stephen told all about the . He said

their families killed prophets who said

 would come. He said these themselves

had killed They were very angry! Stephen

looked to and saw the glory of God and

 standing at the right of God. The

threw . Stephen , "Lord , receive

my spirit. Do not hold this sin against them." After

he said that, he died and went to .

What Did You Learn?

Jesus is with us as we bravely tell others about him.

A Clever Escape

Acts 9:20–25

Saul, who was also called Paul, was cruel to

Christians. Then **1** day a light blinded him. He heard

 speak and believed in . After God

Jesus   Jesus

healed his , Saul began to preach that

eyes   Jesus

is the Son of God. who heard him were

People

amazed. They asked, "Isn't he the who caused

man

trouble for Christians? Has he come here to take

them to ?" Yet Saul proved to them that

jail

is the Christ. Some plotted to kill Saul,

but he learned of their plan. Day and they kept

close watch on the gates of the so they could

kill him as he came out. But one his friends

lowered him in a through

an opening in the of

the .

What Did You Learn?

Tell others about Jesus
even if it's risky.

113

An Earthquake Shakes the Jail

Acts 16:16–40

Paul and Silas were beaten and thrown into .
jail

Instead of , they and hymns to God!
crying   prayed   sang

An earthquake shook the . The flew open,
jail   doors

and everybody's chains came loose. The jailer was

 he would be in big trouble if prisoners escaped.
afraid

Paul shouted, "We are all here!" The jailer fell in
down

front of Paul and Silas. He asked, "What must I do to be

saved?" They said, "Believe in the Lord , and
Jesus

you will be saved." The jailer and his family were

baptized. He was very  happy his whole family believed

in God. In the morning, leaders told him to let Paul

and Silas go free.

What Did You Learn?

Praise God in every situation.
He can turn what's bad
into good.

Falling Out the Window

Acts 20:7–12

One  (night), (people) who believed in  (Jesus) had a

meeting. A young (man) named Eutychus sat in a third-

story (window) listening to Paul talk. Paul talked for a

long, long time until midnight. The young man's

 (eyes) began to close. He sank into a deep sleep and

fell out the (window) (down) to the (ground). When they

picked him (up), he was dead! Paul went (down) the

 (stairs), threw himself on the young (man), and put his

116

arms around him. "Don't be 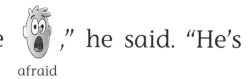," he said. "He's
afraid

alive!" They were that Eutychus was alive. Then
happy

they all went back the , ate ,
up   stairs   bread

and listened to Paul talk until the  rose.
sun

What Did You Learn?

God can do great things through
people who trust him.

Shipwrecked!

Acts 27

While Paul was in  jail , he and other prisoners

had to go to Italy by boat . A terrible storm arose. The

people were afraid . Paul said to them, "An angel told

me not **1** of you will be lost; only the boat will be

destroyed." The boat ran into a sandbar, and the

back part of the boat was broken to pieces by the

waves. Some men jumped into the water to swim

to land. The rest got there on wooden planks or

pieces of the boat . Everyone was safe!

What Did You Learn?

When we're in danger,
we can trust God.

What's Biting You?

Acts 28:1–6

After the shipwreck, Paul and the others swam or floated to shore in the cold . The nice on the island built a . As Paul put wood on

rain people fire

the , a poisonous  came out of the

fire snake

wood and bit Paul! When the saw the

people

 hanging from Paul's , they thought

snake hand

Paul was being punished for doing something

. But Paul just shook the  off into the

wrong snake

fire

. Paul did not swell or die. He was fine.

up

Then thought he was a god. Of course, Paul

people

was not a god, and the people should have

 the real God who saved him instead!

worshiped

What Did You Learn?

The devil attacks us when we're down,
but God helps us survive.

God's Amazing Grace

John 3:16; 23–25; 14:6–7; Romans 5:8;
Ephesians 2:8–10; 1 John 2:3–6, 9–10

God's grace is the undeserved kindness he shows us.

Because God us, he offers us a way to

loves

 . Jesus said, "I am the way ... No **1** comes to

heaven

the Father except through me." We sin when we do

 things and also when we do what is

wrong   do not

good and . Sin could have kept us out of

right

 . But because of his grace, God let

heaven   Jesus

take punishment for our sins on the . God

cross

loved

the so much that he gave his **1** and
world

only Son so whoever believes in will not die
Jesus

but will live forever in  .
heaven

What Did You Learn?

Because of God's amazing grace,
he sent Jesus to be the way
for us to go to heaven.

Dressed in Armor

Ephesians 6:10–17

Be 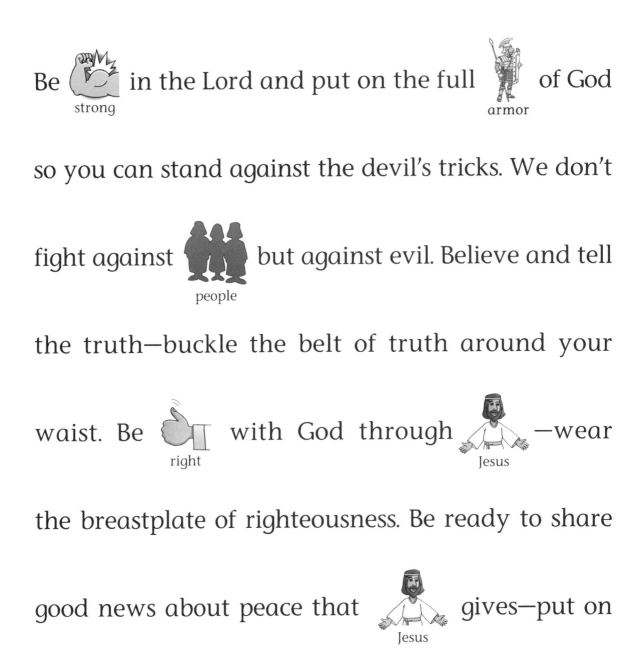 **strong** in the Lord and put on the full **armor** of God

so you can stand against the devil's tricks. We don't

fight against **people** but against evil. Believe and tell

the truth—buckle the belt of truth around your

waist. Be **right** with God through **Jesus**—wear

the breastplate of righteousness. Be ready to share

good news about peace that **Jesus** gives—put on

readiness shoes. Believe God—hold a shield of faith

124

against temptations the devil shoots like fiery

arrows. Trust to save you—wear a of

Jesus   helmet

salvation. Remember the Word of God—fight the

devil with the  of the Spirit.

sword

What Did You Learn?

Be strong in the Lord
  so we're ready
to fight temptations.

We're the Body of Christ

1 Corinthians 12; Ephesians 4:1–16

God gives his Holy Spirit to people who believe in

Jesus
. The Holy Spirit gives us the power to serve

God. Just like feet ,  hands , eyes , and ears

work together in a body, believers with different

abilities work together for Jesus. The eye can't say to

the hand , "I don't need you!" Christians need each

other very much. If **1** part suffers, every part suffers

with it. If **1** part is honored, every part is happy with it. Every believer is an important part of the body

of Christ, and Jesus is the head. As each part does its

work, the body grows in .

love

What Did You Learn?

Christians need to work together
like parts of a body.

We're Going Up in the Air

Matthew 24:36–44; 25:1–30; Mark 13:32–37;
Luke 12:35–56; 21:34–36; 1 Thessalonians 4:16–18

When (Jesus) went (up) to (heaven) in the  (clouds),

 (angels) told the (people) there that (Jesus) would return

the same way. (Jesus) said he will come back when no **1**

expects him. Even the (angels) (do not) know the exact

day or hour. A (trumpet) will sound when (Jesus) comes

 (down) from (heaven). (People) who died believing in him will

rise (up) first. After that, believers who are still alive

will catch (up) with them in the  (clouds) to meet (Jesus)

in the air and to be with (Jesus) forever!

What Did You Learn?

Jesus wants us to be ready
for his return.

Subject Index